A Benjamin Blog
and his Inquisitive Dog
Guide

Republic of Ireland

Anita Ganeri

raintree

a Capstone company — publishers for children

Raintree is an imprint of Capstone Global Library Limited, a company incorporated in England and Wales having its registered office at 7 Pilgrim Street, London, EC4V 6LB – Registered company number: 6695582

www.raintree.co.uk
myorders@raintree.co.uk

Edited by Helen Cox Cannons and Tony Wacholtz
Designed by Steve Mead
Original illustrations © Capstone Global Library Limited 2015
Illustrated by Sernur ISIK
Picture research by Svetlana Zhurkin
Production by Helen McCreath
Originated by Capstone Global Library Limited
Printed and bound in China by CTPS

ISBN 978 1 406 29089 9
18 17 16 15 14
10 9 8 7 6 5 4 3 2 1

British Library Cataloguing in Publication Data
A full catalogue record for this book is available from the British Library.

Acknowledgements
We would like to thank the following for permission to reproduce photographs: Alamy: Mikel Bilbao Gorostiaga Travels, 6; Dreamstime: Fr3ank33, 12; iStockphotos: martinturzak, 20, sharynos, 14; Newscom: Arco Images G/picture alliance/W. Dieterich, 7, Danita Delimont Photography/William Sutton, 25, Design Pics/George Munday, 8, Design Pics/The Irish Image Collection, 26, Robert Harding/Jeremy Lightfoot, 23, World History Archive, 27, 29; Shutterstock: Andrei Nekrassov, 13, Andres Ello, 9, AridOcean, 5, Eoghan McNally, 22, Javier Soto Vazquez, 11, Martina I. Meyer, 24, MShev, 21, Patryk Kosmider, 18, Paul Stringer, 28, Peter Fuchs, cover, SandyS, 19, Stuart Monk, 15, Thierry Maffeis, 17, Wesley Cowpar, 10; Stockbyte, 4; SuperStock: Hemis.fr, 16.

Every effort has been made to contact copyright holders of material reproduced in this book. Any omissions will be rectified in subsequent printings if notice is given to the publisher.

Some words are shown in bold, **like this.** You can find out what they mean by looking in the glossary.

Contents

Welcome to the Republic of Ireland! . . 4

Story of Ireland 6

Coasts, cliffs and mountains 8

City streets 12

Dia duit! 14

Time for dinner 20

Good *craic* 22

From cows to crystal 24

And finally 26

Ireland fact file 28

Ireland quiz 29

Glossary 30

Find out more 31

Index 32

Welcome to the Republic of Ireland!

Hello! My name's Benjamin Blog and this is Barko Polo, my **inquisitive** dog. (He's named after ancient ace explorer, **Marco Polo**.) We have just got back from our latest adventure – exploring the Republic of Ireland. We put this book together from some of the blog posts we wrote on the way.

NORTHERN IRELAND

REPUBLIC OF IRELAND

Dublin

Limerick

Cork

BARKO'S BLOG-TASTIC IRELAND FACTS

Ireland is an island in the Atlantic Ocean, off the
west coast of Great Britain. The north-east corner of
the island is called Northern Ireland and is part of
the United Kingdom. The rest of the island is called
the Republic of Ireland.

Story of Ireland

Posted by: Ben Blog | 21 December at 12 noon

Our first stop in Ireland was Newgrange, an amazing **tomb** built more than 5,000 years ago. It was carefully designed so that, on the shortest day of the year (that's today), the sun shines through a hole above the door straight into the main burial chamber. What a sight!

From 1845 to 1851, a **famine** struck Ireland. A disease killed the potato crop that many people relied on for food. Around a million people died and millions more left Ireland. This statue in Dublin remembers that terrible time.

Coasts, cliffs and mountains

Posted by: Ben Blog | 10 January at 1.56 p.m.

We're now on the Blasket Islands, off the south-west coast of Ireland. The wind is very strong here. People used to live on these islands but, with no electricity or running water, life was very tough. In 1953, the last islanders moved to the **mainland**, leaving their homes behind.

BARKO'S BLOG-TASTIC IRELAND FACTS

Peat bogs cover large parts of Ireland. They are home to lots of different plants, such as sphagnum moss, bog rosemary and sundews, like these beauties, that trap insects to eat.

Staying in the west of Ireland, I set off to climb Carrauntoohil. At 1,038 metres (3,406 feet) tall, it is the highest mountain in Ireland and is part of a mountain range called Macgillycuddy's Reeks. It is a bit of a trek up to the big metal cross that marks the top.

BARKO'S BLOG-TASTIC IRELAND FACTS

This is the Burren, a huge, rocky pavement in County Clare. It is criss-crossed by deep, jagged cracks. These are called grykes and are made by water wearing the rock away.

City streets

Posted by: Ben Blog | 9 February at 6.45 p.m.

From Carrauntoohil, we headed east to Dublin. It is the biggest city in Ireland and the capital city. Barko took this snap of O'Connell Bridge, which crosses the River Liffey. The river flows through the centre of the city. We're off to Dublin Castle next.

BARKO'S BLOG-TASTIC IRELAND FACTS

Ireland's second largest city is Cork, in the south. This is the old Cork City Gaol (say "jail"). You can visit a cell and see what life was like for criminals in the 1800s. Very grim indeed.

Dia duit!

Posted by: Ben Blog | 1 March at 10.01 a.m.

About 4.6 million people live in Ireland. Most people speak English, but some people also speak Irish. In Irish, *Dia duit* means "hello". Irish is mostly spoken in the west, and children have to learn it at school. There are also Irish-language stations on TV and radio.

BARKO'S BLOG-TASTIC IRELAND FACTS

Over the last 175 years, many people have left Ireland to live and work in other countries, such as England, the United States and Canada. They have taken their Irish traditions with them.

In Ireland, most children start school when they are five years old. Most schools teach the children in English, but some schools teach them in Irish. In some places, schools are very small. One school on the island of Inishturk has only two teachers and seven pupils.

It is St Patrick's Day – the biggest celebration in Ireland. We're here in Limerick, with a huge crowd, to watch the grand parade. St Patrick is the patron saint of Ireland. Legend says that he was captured by pirates and brought to Ireland as a slave when he was 16 years old.

Most people in Ireland are Christians. Many belong to the **Roman Catholic Church**. This Christian **monastery** was built on the island of Skellig Michael around 1,400 years ago.

Time for dinner...

Posted by: Ben Blog | 17 March at 7.56 p.m.

After a long, tiring day, we were hungry, so we stopped off for some food. I wanted something filling, so I had a big bowl of Irish stew. It is a stew made from lamb, potatoes, carrots, onions and parsley. It was very tasty, but I couldn't eat another mouthful.

BARKO'S BLOG-TASTIC IRELAND FACTS

Barmbrack is sweet bread with raisins and sultanas. At Halloween, things are hidden inside, such as a coin and a ring. If you get a slice with the coin, it means that you are going to be rich!

Good *craic*

Posted by: Ben Blog | 18 August at 3.30 p.m.

Back in Dublin, we're at Croke Park to watch a Gaelic football match. Gaelic football is the most popular sport in Ireland. Players can kick, bounce or throw the ball. The two teams playing today are Offaly and Westmeath. There's so much noise!

BARKO'S BLOG-TASTIC IRELAND FACTS

This band is playing traditional Irish music. Irish musicians often play **fiddles**, whistles and drums. The music is lively and catchy, and you can't help singing and dancing along.

From cows to crystal

Posted by: Ben Blog | 2 October at 3.34 p.m.

Ireland has rich soil and plenty of rain, which means that grass grows well. Animals such as cows and sheep graze on the grass. Cows are kept for their meat and milk. The milk is also turned into butter and cheese. Farmers also grow crops, such as wheat, oats and **sugar beet**.

BARKO'S BLOG-TASTIC IRELAND FACTS

The city of Waterford in south-east Ireland is famous for making a special type of glass called crystal. The glass is blown into shape and used to make vases, glasses, clocks and even huge **chandeliers**.

And finally...

Our last stop was Blarney Castle, near Cork. At the top of one of its towers is a block of stone, called the Blarney Stone. Legend says that if you kiss the stone, you will get the **gift of the gab**. But you have to hang upside down over the **battlements** to reach the stone. Yikes!

BARKO'S BLOG-TASTIC IRELAND FACTS

The Book of Kells in Trinity College, Dublin, was written by Christian **monks** around 1,300 years ago. It contains part of the Bible and is illustrated with beautiful pictures. It is one of Ireland's most precious treasures.

Ireland fact file

Area: 70,273 square kilometres
  (27,133 square miles)

Population: 4,832,765 (2014)

Capital city: Dublin

Other main cities: Cork, Galway, Limerick

Languages: English, Irish

Main religion: Roman Catholicism

Highest mountain: Carrauntoohil
  (1,041 metres/3,415 feet)

Longest river: Shannon (386 kilometres/240 miles)

Currency: Euro

Ireland quiz

Find out how much you know about Ireland with our quick quiz.

1. Which is the highest mountain in Ireland?
a) Ben Nevis
b) Scafell Pike
c) Carrauntoohil

2. Which river flows through Dublin?
a) Shannon
b) Liffey
c) Bann

3. What does *Dia duit* mean?
a) hello
b) goodbye
c) how are you?

4. When is St Patrick's Day?
a) 16 March
b) 18 March
c) 17 March

5. What is this?

Answers
1. c
2. b
3. a
4. c
5. the Book of Kells

Glossary

battlement stepped wall around the top of a castle

chandelier decorative light fixture that hangs down from the ceiling

craic Irish word for having a good time and a chat with friends

famine time when people starve to death because there is not enough food

fiddle another name for a violin

gift of the gab able to speak well and cleverly

inquisitive interested in learning about the world

mainland main part of a landmass

Marco Polo explorer who lived from about 1254 to 1324. He travelled from Italy to China.

monastery place where monks live and worship

monk man who devotes his life to worshipping God

peat material found in the ground that is mainly made of rotting plants

Roman Catholic Church part of the Christian Church

sugar beet plant whose roots are used to produce sugar

tomb place where dead bodies are buried

Find out more

Books

Ireland (Countries Around the World), Melanie Waldron (Raintree, 2012)

United Kingdom (Countries in Our World), Michael Burgan (Franklin Watts, 2013)

United Kingdom (Discover Countries), Tim Atkinson (Wayland, 2013)

Websites

kids.nationalgeographic.co.uk/kids/places/find
National Geographic's website has lots of information, photos and maps of countries around the world.

http://www.timeforkids.com/destination/ireland
This website gives facts about Ireland and includes a history timeline and sightseeing guide.

www.worldatlas.com
Packed with information about different countries, this website has flags, time zones, facts and figures, maps and timelines.

Index

barmbrack 21
Blarney Stone 26
Blasket Islands 8
Book of Kells 27
Burren 11

Carrauntoohil 10, 28
cities 12–13, 25, 28
Cork 13

Dublin 12, 17, 22

famine 7
farming 24
food 20–21

Gaelic football 22
glass blowing 25

history 6–7

Irish stew 20
islands 5, 8, 16, 19

languages 14

mountains 10, 28
music 23

Newgrange 6
Northern Ireland 5

peat bogs 9
people 14–15, 28
plants 9

religion 19
Republic of Ireland 5
rivers 12, 28

St Patrick's Day 18
schools and universities
   16–17
Skellig Michael 19
sport 22

Trinity College 17, 27

Waterford 25